ISLAND FLIGHT

ISLAND FLIGHT

A True Story

Sophia Gerakis Gemelas

authorHOUSE®

AuthorHouse™
1663 Liberty Drive
Bloomington, IN 47403
www.authorhouse.com
Phone: 1-800-839-8640

First published by AuthorHouse   08/11/2011

ISBN: 978-1-4634-3156-3 (sc)
ISBN: 978-1-4634-3154-9 (ebk)

Library of Congress Control Number: 2011911942

Printed in the United States of America

Any people depicted in stock imagery provided by Thinkstock are models, and such images are being used for illustrative purposes only.
Certain stock imagery © Thinkstock.

This book is printed on acid-free paper.

Sophia G. Gemelas
4803 Forest Edge Drive
Brooklyn, OH 44144
(216) 661-1683

1

A Dream

Six—year—old George stood barefoot on the rocky beach of Ikaria, a mountainous ninety-nine square mile island of Ikaria, Greece, looking down at the rocks and boulders through the clear, sparkling water of the Aegean Sea. Slowly, he lifted his eyes and saw the glistening specks, like diamonds, shimmering across the vast sea, ending at the horizon. He took in the beauty of this breathtaking seascape with a longing sigh. He saw boats and ships passing by to unknown destinations. Because of his bleak existence, he thought there must be something better at the beyond. He dreamed of leaving this place on one of those boats or ships.

His daydreaming came to a screeching halt with the loud bleat of the sheep he attended, in as much as taking care of the needs of a dozen sheep comprised one of his chores. He loved his animals and had to be sure the herd did not graze on the neighbors' fields. His hunger nudged him to take out an onion, a few olives and a small piece of bread, about the size of his palm, from a bag in his pocket. This rationed food was all he had to eat the whole day. He dunked the bread in the salty sea to moisten it, took a couple of bites, and then he put the rest back in his pocket for later. When the ewes had baby lambs in the spring, they nursed their young for three months, and either George or his father tied a sack over the ewe's udders so the lambs could not nurse anymore. At this time the lambs were sold to get money for food such as flour, salt, and sugar, thus for the next two months George drew milk from the udders into a cup, and he would dunk the dry bread in this cup of milk. At other times, he squirted the milk right into his mouth; albeit, this scant nourishment endured him all day as cheese, eggs, or leftovers did not exist for him, and meat was non-existent, except once in a while, when a pig was slaughtered. Neighbors brought their female pigs to mate with the male pig, and in return they gave a piglet to George's father. Then George's father grew this runt until such time that he could slaughter it and finally have some meat again.

Today when it was time to take the herd to the water hole, George tied and led one of the sheep; consequently, the rest followed, but the weary flock traveled a long distance to the watering spot and fatigued easily. George knew of a closer source in a ravine, and he took his 5-year old brother, Nick, to accompany him. Of course, Nick did not have any shoes either, and as they climbed down the rocky slopes, the burrs pricked and stuck to their feet. Compelled by the discomfort and pain, they stopped, removed them, and walked on the gravel and rocks to avoid the burrs; however; the rocks cut into their feet. To stop the bleeding, they applied dry sheep manure on the nicks and wounds, and then washed their feet in the salty water of the sea. In the winter there were no burrs, but they still suffered from the cold. Down they went on makeshift paths as they passed boulder after boulder. The animals could not reach this winter water hole pooled below one of the huge rocks, so George crawled in between the boulders, and his brother lowered a pail for him to fill up with the water. When it was filled, George signaled Nick, and slowly and carefully, Nick pulled the bucket up and the animals drank from the pail.

That spring George intended to rope one of the sheep to lead the herd. The sheep had other ideas as she stared at George when he approached. This was a burly, thick white-woolen sheep with an attitude. She already had pushed George before, and again jostled him and caused him to fall head first down the slope. This time she ran away, but George quickly got up to his feet and chased her on the hilly, rocky, terrain where his barefoot slid on a pebble laying on one of the rocks. Consequently, he fell backwards, hurt his back, and for the next fifteen days he walked in pain with a makeshift bamboo cane.

2

Recovery at Home

The home George recuperated in was originally one room, which his grandfather received as dowry when he married. His grandfather eventually tore it down and then rebuilt it with stones cemented together with mud. The second layer of stones overlapped the first, and a slate roof covered the structure. The rats ate through the mud all the way up to the second floor which created a passage way for the snakes and scorpions to take up residence, too. His grandparents and eight children, born without the care of a doctor or midwife, lived in the one room on the second floor that housed two beds. Now George's parents and four children occupied the home. Four boys, George and his three younger brothers, slept in one iron-framed bed with circular, hollow posts, with the mattress made up of burlap sacks filled with corn husks, and covered with goat skin. The storage area of the dirt floor on the first level contained vats of olive oil, potatoes, onions that were braided and hung on the walls, along with tools. His father had previously brought a loom from America when he was single, and now George's mother weaved cloth from sheep's wool and made blankets. A neighbor, who knew how to sew, once made jackets for the boys, but this was a one-time deal as the boys outgrew them.

The kitchen accommodated a fireplace; however, lack of a sink, running water and furniture, except for the small, round, eighteen—inches high and three—foot diameter table, and wooden stools George's father made for chairs, which created a dismal, barren area. A hole in the wall, covered with a curtain, served as the cupboard. To get water for the basin outside the house that served as the sink, George went to a neighbor's well, lowered his pail into it, pulled it up and carried it to the house. When there was no water to wash the pot, George's father just turned it over and the next day cooked in the unwashed pot again. Absence of any dishes forced everyone, including visitors, to eat out of one clay pot with rusty forks or spoons. The children repeatedly argued over who would use one of these precious utensils, a favorite small, corroded, rusty fork. His mother fed up with the bickering, took the little fork, bent it, broke it, and then threw it away.

The toilet was an outhouse built on one of the terraces, recessed about three feet into the dirt wall, with three walls of stone and no door surrounding this private space. The non-existent bench forced the occupants to squat. One day in the outhouse, a startled George faced a writhing snake that had suddenly reared its ugly head out of the ground. No means of escape remained except to yell that a snake terrorized him, and his father came running with a shotgun. The six-foot creature would never bother anyone again after that. In the winter, it was too cold to go outside at night to use this facility, so the ingenious boys would relieve themselves in the iron, hollow bed posts. Of course, the stench betrayed them, and George's mother had to disassemble the whole bed to clean it, and the boys received a spanking.

George's mother always nagged his father because of their poverty, and on an Easter day, George's father went to church in the morning and returned to tend to the animals. From the second story, George saw his father buttoning his shirt as his mother's relentless nagging chipped away at his father's patience, to the point that his father grasped the shotgun off the wall. At this point George's mother chased him away, so that George did not know what happened after that.

Scorpions also had their way with George, as a scorpion stung one of his bare feet when he walked one night with his mother. His lips became numb, and pain riddled his whole body for the next twenty-four hours. Another time he bent over to reach into a deep vat of dried figs, and instead of retrieving a fig, he pulled out a scorpion attached to his finger; and same symptoms occurred afresh.

Other chores awaited George. At the age of seven years old, in 1931, he made bread as his mother had gone to Athens, the capital of Greece, nine hours away by boat, to see a doctor. She took with her the youngest brother, Spiro, age two, and was absent for three months. George was left with his father and two other brothers, Nick, age six, and four-year—old Gus. Still, being the oldest of four boys at that time, he had the responsibility to care for them while his father tended the fields and sheep. To make bread, George put approximately thirty pounds of flour, some salt and water in a mammoth pan, and then kneaded the dough with all his might, as much as he could, to make big round loaves. He had watched his mother when she baked, and his curiosity compelled him to ask questions such as why the oven turned red. She said, "When the brick lining the outdoor oven changes from red to white, the oven is ready to bake the bread at the right temperature."

The arch-shaped, brick oven had a loose, huge slab of stone for a door. He placed his loaves on a wooden flat shovel, like a giant tennis racket, and shoved the bread into the oven and quickly closed the door, so the oven would not cool off. Water seeped into the rear of the oven, and consequently, the back of the bread baked unevenly. To remedy this, George stood the partially brown bread on the edge against the wall of the oven, and left it there to bake until well done.

Nick and Gus were too young to lend a hand, so they just played with one another and were of no help to George. As if all these chores were not enough, George also did the rest of cooking. He boiled potatoes, greens, and sometimes when his father went fishing and caught fish, he and his father fried or boiled the fish in clay pots placed over an open flame in the fireplace. Usually the smoke filled the room to the point that George and his brothers had to crawl on the ground to be able to breathe.

Still, more tasks had to be done, by the time he was 10, George laundered the clothes, while his mother and father worked in the fields. He fetched water pail by pail from a well, boiled it over an open fire, then poured it into a huge tub and repeated this process until the tub filled. After that, he scrubbed the clothes by hand with hand-made olive-oil soap. This was hard for him, as the clothes were heavy, stiff, and covered with caked-on dirt. To alleviate his duties, George ordered Nick and Gus to gather fodder for the huge, 1,000 pound pig they had, but the brothers resented him giving orders and did not obey. Then George got in a fight with them, and they ran to his mother, who in turn came after George, but he ran up the slope and sat under a cypress tree looking out at the sea again wondering how he could leave this place.

Amidst all of this, moments of fun and play abounded. George had no toys, but he played tag and hide and seek with the other children in the marble churchyard, as no other play area existed. However, the priest chased them away, as they made too much noise, and he even slapped George as he stood on the steps; on the other hand, when the priest could not catch them to inflict corporal punishment, he threw his cane at them, so George found another course of entertainment. He flung flat rocks across the water and counted how many times they merrily skipped on the waves. In the summertime, he tied the larger sheep to a tree, and the smaller sheep and lambs stayed close by. Then he swam in the warm, clear, blue water of the Aegean Sea. He learned to swim previously when he stood on top of a large boulder as an older friend had instructed him to do. The friend then told him to jump in the water, as he watched him. Afraid, and apprehensive, but determined to learn, George trusted him and jumped in quickly before he lost his resolve. "Use your arms and legs!" his friend shouted. George knew how to float and finally gained confidence as he thrashed about in the water. For another pastime, he picked up a spider and wrapped her web over and over around his hands, as he marveled at the unending supply of strands. Also, he and his brothers, as well as other children in the village, cut bamboo shoots from a neighbor's yard, and made recorders, a musical wind instrument. They were told not to do this, as the bamboo was used to make baskets, hats, furniture, window shades, canes, and also layered on roofs as a base with plaster and slate covering it.

Annoyed by their repeated actions, George's mother, in order to frighten them, tied all four to a tree and set fire to bushes, at a safe distance, surrounding them. However, the children knew this was a scare tactic and continued to take the bamboo.

3

School Days

When George attended school, he and one hundred sixty children occupied the one-room, stone schoolhouse, wherein long benches performed the duty of desks for six classes, grades one through six. In 1930, a new school was constructed with stone again, but with a ceramic roof, two rooms, and a small office for the one teacher. This time two pupils sat at a desk and faced a chalkboard and a single map of Greece. The lone teacher taught grades one through six, and while he instructed one grade, the other classes sat silently studying. Not a whisper could be heard, as the teacher invoked corporal punishment and had a switch from an olive tree that he used to maintain order. George felt the sting and pain of this switch, not for misbehaving, but because he did not know the lesson. If the teacher disciplined a student, then that pupil got a second, worse punishment at home from his parents. One time when George attempted a futile effort to solve a math problem at the board, the teacher kicked him and hurled him across the room. George felt utter embarrassment and disgrace and awaited a harsher outcome at home.

Two or three books were supplied to each grade level, and these belonged to children who could buy their books and materials, notebooks, pencil, eraser, a slate and chalk, as they had relatives in the United States who sent them money. The teacher had his own book and allowed those students without books to use his when reading, unless that student sat next to someone who had a book and shared with him. Needless to say, only a few affluent students had pencils, paper, and notebooks to take notes and study at home. George did not have the luxury of owning his own book and supplies, because of his poverty predicament and consequently, he learned mostly by auditory means.

The school sessions occurred during the day only, as electricity arrived in the future, and kerosene lamps emitted light exclusively at home. Non-existent heat cast a chill among the students, and George shivered with no jacket or shoes. An old stove sat quietly in the corner of the room, and during extremely cold days, the teacher asked the students to bring in twigs to light it. After school, George hurried home and attended to the animals. To get to the high school, located in the capital of Ikaria, required two hours walking each way. Students rented a room, paid tuition, bought their books, supplies, and, of course, their meals; however, lack of monetary means precluded George from attending.

4

Working Days

Finally, when George finished elementary school at age 12, he went to work for an older lady in another village, Arethousa, high up in the mountain. His grandmother and aunt knew this lady who lived alone and needed help to take care of her animals. They proposed George to her, so he went to work for her as a farm boy. His job required him to tend to the animals including a donkey with her baby donkey, goats, sheep and chickens. His salary of 100 drachmas a month was insufficient to buy a pair of trousers or pair of shoes, and his patched pants challenged anyone to decipher which was the original material. His grandmother slept at the lady's house and kept her company. They ate well: cheese, eggs, olives and drank milk, but for George, who left at dawn and returned at nightfall, the lady supplied him with a piece of stale bread and a few olives for his meals for the whole day. Needless to say, he was always hungry.

The free—roaming chickens laid their eggs anywhere, and while doing his job, George found a hen's nest with about a dozen eggs in it. He dutifully gave the eggs to the lady, but she did not give him any to eat. A second time he found another nest with eggs in it and again turned them over to the lady, but still, she did not reward him with any. A third time he found some more eggs, and this time he put them in a metal can he had in his goatskin backpack, added water to the can, built a fireplace using stones, then lit a fire. He cooked the eggs and feasted for the first time on this special dinner. This is no life he thought, as he ate, being barefoot, hungry, tired and disgusted, so he finally left without remuneration and came back to his village. He went to the seashore and gazed out at the open sea once more. He watched the waves caress and then slap the rocks and boulders. He wondered if he would ever leave this poverty-stricken, mountainous island.

5

Starvation

No paying jobs existed for George's father or mother, and since they had no land by their house, except for a six to ten foot terrace, they cleared their fields in Vaoni, a half-hour walk from their house, and also the neighbors' fields, before the rains came in the fall. They were allowed to use the neighbor's fields, for doing so was better to cultivate the land than to let bushes and shrubs grow wild. They harnessed the neighbor's cows to till the soil, planted crops and tended the animals. Since they were all barefoot, they suffered broken toe nails and cuts, so they applied the animal manure to stop the bleeding, then soaked their feet in the salty sea to clean and disinfect the wounds. They also fished at the shore with bamboo fishing poles, and if they caught a big fish, took it to the village grocer, exchanged it for food such as cheese, rice, flour, salt, sugar and other staples, and his mother made noodles and spaghetti by hand.

George, his parents and brothers had so little to eat in 1935. His father sailed to the mainland of Greece for six months for a job making charcoal, a black, soft substance, made by burning wood and used as fuel. In the meantime his mother and brothers gathered dandelions and other edible greens and cooked them in one big pot, which they all ate out of with some dried bread and olive oil. Usually no other food accompanied their meals except for gathered stems with thorns, which they picked off then boiled them. They grew some wheat, reaped the wheat, gathered the stalks, bound them in sheaves, and took them to a mill on a hot day, so the stalks broke more easily. This removed the chaff, and then they waited for the wind to blow away the chaff. After that, they washed the wheat, waited about twenty days for it to dry, and George and Nick turned a mill to grind it. They did this for most of the day, and they were exhausted from toiling and from hunger to the point that they could not go on any longer. They and their younger brothers languished on the ground, and his mother carried one child at a time and transported him a distance away and came back to carry another. An older neighbor going up the steep slope, saw their plight, and asked what was the matter. When George's mother told him that her children were starving, he said he thought he had something, went into his house, came out and gave her a handful of orzo, a rice-shaped pasta. She boiled it, fed the children, and they sprung up as if they were given an energy injection.

This existence continued for several more years, and in November 1939, when George turned 15 years old, he worked for two months at an olive grove on an oil press, converting olives into oil in his village of Chrisostomos. He gathered olives, and then turned a marble cylinder by hand to press the olives into a mush. After this, he placed the mush on towels, with the four corners folded toward the middle, and arranged it on a hand press to squeeze out the oil. It took him two weeks to produce a thirty—pound can of oil. His pay was one kilogram, equal to about 2.2 pounds, of oil that he generated from dawn to dusk. He sold this at Agios Kirikos, the capital, and went to Samos, another island which had jurisdiction over Ikaria. Here he filled out the necessary papers to get a permit to sail on the boats or ships. Ships are ocean-going vessels, with a displacement larger than 500 tons and over 300 feet in length, whereas boats tend to be much smaller and less than 300 feet in length. For the first time, George believed dreams do come true, and wondered if this portal would lead to a better place.

6

New Adventures

In 1940, George went to the seaport, Piraeus, on the southeast mainland of Greece, and got a job on a 100-ton wooden pine caique (pronounced ka`eek), a light skiff or small boat that had no toilets, so that the sailors held onto the ropes and voided in the sea. He worked as a cook and steered the boat, but being a novice at this, he steered too close to the shore, and the captain slapped him. Eventually he made his way to the island Chios in the Aegean Sea not far from Ikaria, about two or three hours' trip, and loaded oranges, bound for Piraeus. He could eat as many oranges as he wanted; unfortunately, the captain sold the caique, and dismissed George. Again, in Piraeus, he was able to connect with another smaller, ten—to fifteen—ton, caique bound for Missolonghi, a city on the Gulf of Patras, an inlet of Ioanian Sea, west of Greece, to load feta, a white cheese. The captain brought in a passenger, who slept on the floor on George's bedding. The owners and captains had their own cabins, and the crew, mainly George, slept on the floor between the cabins. The worst part for George occurred when the passenger attempted to get bold and disrespectful of him, trying to touch George and see what his response would be. George pulled away and moved as far away as he could, faced the passenger and did not dare turn his back to him. The elusive sleep inhibited a good night's rest for George, as he remembered his mother's advice. She said, "My child, wherever you sojourn in foreign places, you will meet good people, but also bad people so, be aware and alert." The passenger was very generous with his lice, which he shared with George.

During the Easter season, the captain discharged George without notice; thus the captain avoided paying insurance and pension for him. Naive about shipping regulations, George just accepted this, not knowing that the captain was liable for breaking the law; and subject to prosecution. Nevertheless, he found himself in Piraeus again without work, but this time infested with lice. He went to an aunt in Athens and asked her to boil his clothes to get rid of the lice, but she threw the clothes away. To add to his plight, he had no underwear to wear, but for the first time in his life, he had real shoes and new clothes he purchased with the money he earned.

7

War

World War II, a global military conflict, involved the majority of the world's nations and erupted on September 1, 1939, with the German invasion of Poland; Britain (England) and France entered two days later. The War was primarily fought between two large alliances, namely the Axis powers, a group of countries led by Nazi Germany, Italy and the Empire of Japan, considered the aggressors of the conflict, and the Allies led by the United Kingdom, which consisted of four countries: England, Ireland, Scotland and Wales, and France. The Nazis were members of the National Socialist Workers party, a political party that controlled Germany. The Soviet Union joined the Allies later in

June 1941, and the United States joined in December 1941. The Soviet Union is a short name for the Union of Soviet Socialist Republics (USSR), Communist countries in Eastern Europe and northern Asia that included Russia and fifteen other Soviet Socialist Republics, and officially dissolved on December 31, 1991.

War broke out in Greece in 1940, and impacted George's life when the Italians planned on invading the country from Albania, a country bordering Greece in the Balkan Peninsula on the Adriatic Sea, but the Greek Army fought and held them off in Albania, thus conferring the first victory for the Allies in October 1940. Greece was the only country forced to confront the armies of four countries simultaneously, as they resisted German, Italian, Bulgarian and Albanian attacks for more than seven months. George was proud of the Greeks' bravery and fighting spirit. In April 1941, the mighty German Army came down from Yugoslavia, also bordering Greece, intervened, and the fighting ceased between the Greeks and the Italians. During this time, George, at age 16, found work and sailed on a boat that anchored at St. George, an area close to the Greek Navy base, where ships, before the war, brought in wheat from England, Russia, and other countries to be milled into flour. George looked up at the sky and saw the German airplanes bomb the freighter ships and everything around them. The loud, strident, impact displaced the water in the harbor with such thunderous, tumultuous force that it hurled the boats and ships onto the land. George with trepidation cast his eyes on the battered ships aground as the Greek military shot at the planes with their canons. The booming, deafening, ear-splitting artillery burst in midair, and the falling debris enshrouded the caique. In horror, he also witnessed two German airplanes in flames come screeching to the ground. He felt distressed, depressed and despondent for the pilots and crews who lost their lives so violently.

The Germans occupied Greece in April 1941, when George worked on another ship in Piraeus. He was away from home for a year, and at this time, he learned from another villager that his mother had given birth to a fifth son, John. The defeated, desponded, depressed and displaced Greek soldiers, marching on foot from Albania, were being shipped to Mitilini and other islands. George's boat docked near a bigger vessel, and as a sailor he loaded one hundred soldiers onto the bigger boat. The craft was full, but some weary, way worn, fatigued soldiers approached George and begged him to put them on the departing vessel. Feeling compassion for them, he took three of them and returned to take some more, but the second time he tried to load more men onto the craft, an officer spotted his actions, pulled out his big revolver, pointed it at George and ordered him to take them back to shore, because the boat was overloaded. George was never so unnerved and frightened before in his life, and of course, he complied. He went back to his caique and was afloat in this boat for ten days, as he took in every action on the boat. He observed the battered, beaten, debased, tired, hungry and lice-infested Greek soldiers sleeping on the dirt ground waiting for their turn to go home. The caique docked about ten yards from the pier, so nobody could come on board. George was terrified that the Germans would come after him with their guns, because the skipper had George guard the caique, with the captain's nephew who worked on the engine. The German soldiers wanted the craft, and they wanted the mechanic to take them to the island of Crete, another island south of Greece in the Aegean Sea, as Crete had not yet fallen to the enemy. However, the nephew fled, and the Germans shot at him; but hey missed him and he got away, but George stayed on the boat.

In August, 1941, shipping ceased because of the war, as some vessels were destroyed, sunk, docked, or sailed away and only the small caiques remained, so now George also had to find a way back home to his island. He heard of someone who had a boat headed for Ikaria, and George asked the skipper to take him. He said he would for 1,000 drachmas as fare, and George paid the 1,000 drachmas, his savings of two years. The skipper dropped him off at the wind-beaten harbor less island at the village of Evdilos. A small boat took him to shore, as the whole coastline lacked harbors. From there, he took a small fishing boat and circled the island, to evade detection by the Italian soldiers stationed on the island. He went to Livadi, which was close to his village, and he hid his clothes and belongings in a field. He then climbed the mountain to his village of Chrisostomos, and returned later with his father on his donkey to retrieve his bag and clothes.

8

Escape

U pon his return, George's personal martyrdom began. Now seven people in his family were destitute, as they had little food to eat, for not one day's work existed, and transportation to bring in foodstuffs ceased. The Germans and Italians printed their own currency, which was worthless, and paid the villagers for any goods, or they just simply seized the food and animals for their armies. George's father planted some wheat, and his mother made "paximathe" (bread dried in the oven). For the next seven months, and once a day, one "paximathe" and wild greens with olive oil and olives were rationed for the day. This unhealthy lifestyle engendered malnutrition, and in February

1942, George's 43-year—old father began to swell from
starvation, resulting in edematous, that is, swollen feet
and legs with excessive fluid. Thus, George made the
decision to go to the Middle East, a group of countries
of southwest Asia, as a refugee. His 42-year old mother
cried, because he would be leaving alone, and his father
did not want to move; besides, they were prohibited
from departing the island by the Germans, because it
was war time. Then his mother and siblings also decided
to take the chance to escape, and his mother eventually
persuaded his father to accompany them.

George found a villager who had a 20-foot boat,
and who agreed to take the whole family, along with
seventeen others, to Turkey for 20,000 drachmas.
George's father approached his mother's relatives and
asked for the 20,000 drachmas in exchange for whatever
he had. However, the relatives could not give him the
money, as they needed help more than he did; they also
had nothing.

Then, George's father went to his sister who lived
in the village Arethousa, where George first worked as

a farm boy, and she said she had nothing, even though she had flocks of goats. Finally, two villagers heard of the family's predicament and approached them with a contract to give them the 20,000 drachmas in exchange for all of their possessions. They agreed with the stipulation that when, and if, the family returned, because the Turks would probably force them back, they would return everything except a male sheep, and, of course, his father would repay the 20,000 drachmas.

The family hid the boat in a cove, so the Italians would not see it, and waited for three weeks for the inclement weather to clear. However, the sea was not placated and still angrily churned up the waves. When the storm lulled somewhat, the family finally decided to depart, and each member went one by one at night, gathered their clothes hidden in boughs, branches and in caves, and boarded the boat. Another family with nine children also boarded, so that altogether twenty-four passengers packed the boat under the covered deck, like sardines in a can. Finally, on February 2, 1942, the boat embarked for Turkey in blustery weather; however, while en route, the storm worsened. Instead of sailing southeast, as planned, the weather with fierce, ferocious winds lashing the stern forced the boat to go northeast, while the passengers below prayed. The villagers, who stayed behind on the island, thought the families had drowned; nonetheless, the new boat was in good condition and withstood the squall, as the passengers hovered under the deck, covered with canvas to protect them from the elements.

En route to their destination, the men relieved themselves over the boat, but the women could not. After more than 20 hours, the boat docked at Kato Panagia, a small port in Turkey, but the Turkish authorities ordered them back to Ikaria; they did not want refugees. The skipper's brother acted fast, breaking the steering wheel, and thus precluded the return home. The Turks were angry, so they asked for the captain, and the skipper came forth. They ordered him off the boat, and a Turkish official took off his belt and beat the man, because he brought the refugees.

After that, the Turks ordered everyone ashore, and for them to take the sails and oars to the customs office. They detained the captain for three days, although they fed him and gave him supplies and food to take back to Ikaria. The famished passengers were taken to a town called Tsesmes. A compassionate Turkish soldier carried an infant for about a half hour to this place. Refugees that came after this group informed them that when their captain returned to Ikaria, the Italians beat him and burned his boat, because he executed this escape.

In Turkey, the refugees were housed for one week in a warehouse where they slept on the dirt ground, and lice and bedbugs infested them, as the insects crawled up the walls and ceilings and then dropped down on the people. Here the Turks served bean soup in a huge cauldron, and from a sitting position, everyone ate out of this large kettle, and bean soup became George's favorite food. After about a week, on orders from the British, who controlled the Middle East, the Turks boarded the refugees on a boat bound for Cyprus, another island south of Turkey. The journey took one week and to pass the time, the refugees counted how many lice they killed with their fingernails. The food during this journey consisted of one fig for breakfast, one fig for lunch, and one fig for dinner. Sailing south, the boat encountered warmer weather, and the refugees did not feel cold anymore. En route the boat docked at a beach for a break, and some of the refugees found a goat that fell off the cliff, so they built a fire, cooked the goat and feasted on this delicacy, although George did not partake in this, as he was not part of that group.

While in Cyprus, the Cypriots' hospitality lifted the refugees' spirits. They took the lice infested clothing and gave the refugees sheets and blankets to cover themselves. Then they shaved the men's and children's heads and sprayed them to get rid of the lice. After that, the Cypriots issued new clothes, fed the refugees, gave them medical assistance, and Egyptian currency issued to the adults daily, which bought food for their families.

9

You're in the Army Now

In March 1942, Greek officers from British-ruled Palestine, an ancient region of southwest Asia bordering on the coast of the Mediterranean Sea and extending east of the Jordan River, arrived and ordered all males from age 16 to 60 to step forward. George, his father, age 44, and his brother Nick, age 16, did as they were told. Nick got a deferment for a year, and then was inducted into the Navy, and his father was rejected because of a hand injury. At age 17, George found himself inducted into the Greek Army, specifically the infantry of the Second Brigade. The men sailed to Beirut, a city and port of Lebanon, a country in southwest Asia, bordering on the Mediterranean and from there to Palestine, where uniforms taken off the shelf were issued to the men, regardless of size. Of course, George's oversize uniform on his small stature made him look pathetic, but after a while, the soldiers befriended the clerk, and they exchanged their uniforms for the correct size. The troops lined up for an injection, although George did not know its purpose. He had never even taken a pill before, and he never had an injection previously in his life, so as he approached to receive this shot, he fainted.

For military maneuvers and training, George engaged in physical exercise, target practice, and marched twenty miles in extreme heat, so that his feet blistered and bloodied from the woolen socks and military boots, and he also suffered with a bloody nose. At dinner time an officer ordered the men to gargle first with salt water. George exhausted and hungry, with plate in hand, said, "I don't need to gargle, I need some good food." The astonished officer ordered this insolent soldier to step forward in front of the others, knocked the plate out of George's hand, slapped him and mocked him. He had nothing but scorn for George and treated him with disdain.

The officer shouted, "Look at this puny specimen of a soldier making demands. Twenty days in jail!" Notwithstanding this, the order on record never materialized. Another time, George got sick with a high fever; however, the officer did not believe him and refused to send him to the dispensary. After George agonized for a week, the officer finally believed him and allowed him to go. At this time, George asked for a leave to go to Cyprus to see his family whom he had not seen for a year, and also was denied this request.

In the early 20th century, the British Empire comprised about one quarter of the world's land area and population and encompassed territories on every continent, including British West and East Africa, and these territories came under the rule of the British government. General Bernard Montgomery, one of the British Army's most successful generals, training in warfare, became Field Commander of the Eighth Army in North Africa. He defeated the German Field

Marshal Erwin Rommel at the Battle of El Alamein, in Egypt in 1942, and this victory turned the tide of the war, as the Germans retreated.

The Greek First Brigade fought at this battle, and when they returned to the Middle East at Damascus, Syria, the ordinary soldiers were not permitted to enter establishments that the officers frequented. The English Military Police (MPs) arrested them, but the next day they were released. The Greeks came back, armed this time, and when the MPs confronted them the second time, the Greeks said, "On the battle field we were brothers, but here we are not?" A scuffle ensued and six MPs were killed. From then on, everyone, including George, was allowed in all the establishments. After that, a similar event happened when the Australian and New Zealand soldiers, also under General Montgomery, drank beer, but were forbidden to do so and were incarcerated and then were freed. Inspired by the Greeks, the Australians and New Zealanders got in their tanks; returned and demolished the jail.

In 1943, the Greek Army in the Middle East revolted against King George II of Greece, as they did not want a monarchy in their country. One of the soldiers, a protagonist and leading proponent of the anti-monarchy movement, was shot and killed by another soldier who supported the monarchy. This set off a chain reaction, and a third soldier shot and killed the supporter. The English favored the monarchy and defended the King, a relative of the royal party of England. The English soldiers, under General Montgomery's command, transported the Greeks one company at a time to Tripoli, Syria. The English ordered the Greeks, including George, upon getting off the truck, to lay down their rifles and march a few yards away from their weapons. Three English soldiers manned with machine guns on three mounds pointed their weapons toward the Greek soldiers forcing compliance.

Afterwards aboard trucks, the Greek battalion arrived at an English camp for a thirty-day detention. From there, they traveled to Egypt, a country in Northeast Africa bordering on the Mediterranean and Red Seas, and by train to Tobruk, Libya, a country of North Africa also bordering on the Mediterranean Sea. Here the orders to dig a trench supposedly for garbage disposal seemed reasonable. At the end of the day, the orders to fill up the ditch without dumping garbage in it turned out to be punishment. This directive did not go well with the detainees, so the Greeks refused to be abused and told the English to fill it themselves. The English realized they could not push the Greeks around, and after that they did not bother them.

From Tobruk, the Greeks traveled to Tripoli, Libya for maneuvers and were reinstated as an Army battalion, and from there they returned by railroad again to Tobruk. The English reissued their rifles with orders to guard 12,000 German and Italian prisoners. A few prisoners dug themselves out from under the wire fence and tried to escape. One of them met his fate with a bullet, and the others returned.

Now the Greeks were sent to Benghazi, the second largest city of Libya, for maneuvers. They had the choice to guard the English planes, which bombed other Greeks, "EAM" (Greek Freedom Division) guerrillas, a band of fighters. The EAM was a rigorous resistance movement developed in 1942, by the leftist National Liberation Front, which focused on changing traditional social orders and creating a more egalitarian, that is equal, distribution of wealth. Throughout 1943, the guerrillas succeeded in liberating much of the country's mountainous interior, and after the Italian capitulation in 1943, the Germans took over the Italian zone, accompanied by bloodshed and atrocities. These guerrillas initially fought against the Germans, but now were against the Greek monarchy.

The second option the Greeks had was to transfer to an additional English camp in Asmara, Abyssinia (Ethiopia), another country in Northeast Africa bordering on the Red Sea. At the same time, England sent an army to Athens, the capital of Greece, to fight the guerrillas, or partisans. Those that said "Yes," to guard the planes departed through one exit, and those who refused, through another door. The consenting soldiers were shipped to Rimini, Italy, a port in northern

Italy on the Adriatic Sea, and all were killed in battle by the Germans there.

George declined to guard the airplanes that bombed fellow Greeks, and found himself cramped in a boat's cargo bin in 120—degree heat, and not allowed up for air, bound for a camp in Ethiopia on the Red Sea, sailing first to Alexandria, Egypt and then to Asmara, the capital of Eritrea, a country in Northeast Africa, later incorporated into Ethiopia. This camp confinement lasted for eleven months, albeit the soldiers did not have a difficult time, as they played their instruments, and George learned how to dance, and also learned how to play backgammon. Six soldiers and a sergeant were housed in one tent, and the men drank "eau de vie," a French term for a clear, colorless fruit brandy, strong enough to ignite their exhaled breath with a lit match. George drank the brandy for the first time, got sick, vomited and never tried it again.

A Greek Egyptian in the tent always washed himself and his clothes every morning, and George admired his cleanliness, until George noticed the soldier from

Constantinople (now Istanbul, a city in Northwest Turkey) who slept next to the Egyptian and whose jacket was full of lice, had infected the Egyptian. The detection forced this soldier to place his clothes in a special chamber that disinfested clothes and killed lice and bugs, and thus eliminated this annoyance.

In the summer of 1944, George was delighted with the advance of the Red Army (the Russian Army) through Eastern Europe and with the German forces withdrawal from the Greek mainland in the fall of 1944, although garrisons were left behind on many islands, including Crete where the German forces surrendered on the date May 8, 1945.

On November 22, 1945, George turned twenty-one years old, and on Christmas Eve of that year, he and the rest of the soldiers proceeded on a river boat bound for Alexandria, Egypt, and then back to Tobruk. The English stripped them of their equipment and uniforms, except for the clothes on their backs, and shipped them back to Greece. At this time George had no work, no money and no home, as his family, whom he had not seen for four years, remained in Cyprus, except for his brother, Nick, who was already discharged from the Navy and returned to Ikaria and stayed with an aunt. George went to stay at the aunt's house until spring of that year when the rest of his family returned from Cyprus. Once again, George looked for work on the boats to fulfill a two-year requirement to sail on the big cargo ships.

10

Post War Encounters

Not being able to find work created the next distressing experience for George. However, persistence in his quest for employment paid off. He got his permit to sail on the ships, but it took more than five years to get a job. His family returned from Cyprus empty handed, and as work was unavailable, they went to Vaoni, approximately an eight—acre parcel of land that belonged to the family. Here they burned waste wood and made charcoal which they sold to buy flour and make bread. George made occasional trips to the port Pireaus in pursuit of a job on the ships, and visited fellow villagers on these trips. They introduced him to a young lady, whom he would see on these visits. Her family liked George and wanted him as a son-in-law, so they promised him a dowry of a house if he married her. George agreed, and they were betrothed, with a lavish engagement party. Once in a while, he slept at her house, but was infested with fleas and bed bugs. This disgusted him, and the promised house became a broken promise, so he slowly withdrew from the relationship, and the engagement was broken. The prospective bride asked for her ring back, and George also wanted his ring returned. At a predetermined meeting place, the bride's brother and another man met George. George was wary that they might beat him up because of the dissolution of the affair, and he explained to the brother that he left his sister the way he found her; nonetheless, the brother cried as he knew George was honorable.

A visiting friend, who lived in the Oinoussai Island near Turkey, told George's mother there were many ship-owners there, and she knew of one who needed a cook. George's mother was hired as a chef, but was fired after a month, because she really did not know how to cook. Nevertheless, she made contact with an agent who placed sailors on a ship, for a fee of five gold pounds. His mother borrowed the money from George's godfather, and when the five gold pounds were paid, the agent found George a position.

On George's first trip, he flew to Rotterdam, Holland, a country in Northwest Europe bordering on the North Sea, and boarded the ship, *SS Rhodope*, which transported corn from Germany to England. He navigated the ship, dropped anchor, painted, and opened and closed the cargo hold for a monthly salary of twenty-seven English pounds.

He then sailed to Lisbon, Portugal, a country in Southwest Europe bordering on the Atlantic Ocean, where the crew loaded mineral bound for Rotterdam and covered the cargo bins; however, they did not cover them on Saturday, as the sailors worked half a day according to the law. The owners decided they should work the whole day, but without the time and a half pay they were due, so the crew sent a telegraph to the Greek Embassy informing them of a breach of the law. On Sunday, the officers were in a hurry to depart for

Rotterdam and started to cover the bins themselves; nevertheless, the crew helped them.

When they reached Rotterdam, the consul boarded the ship to settle their differences and being a friend of the captain, the official sided with him. The crew felt justice eluded them, because instead of remuneration for the overtime; he fined each deck hand six pounds. They sailed to Baltimore, unloaded the cargo and returned to Europe; however, the worst awaited them, inasmuch as the sailors' names were listed in documents and sent to the Greek government labeling them as Communists, because they refused to follow orders. George shared this fate with his fellow deck hands, and these blacklisted sailors had difficulty finding work again. Over 150,000 sailors and workers, from other ships and occupations as well, most of them unjustly blacklisted, fled to the Iron Curtain, a physical and ideological division that represented the way Europe was viewed after World War II. To the east of the Iron Curtain were countries that were connected or influenced by the former Soviet Union, including East Germany, Czechoslovakia,

Poland, Hungary, Bulgaria, Romania and Albania. Although George felt upset and despondent, he did not complain about being blacklisted and kept on looking for work.

He connected and sailed on the ship *S.S. Telemon* to Baltimore to unload its cargo. He returned to Greece and worked for one month, but after this, the ship moored at the harbor, for lack of freight to ship. It took George another year to get on one of the Liberty ships, cargo ships built in the United States during World War II made for the war and built for just one trip. They were cheap and quick to build, as they were constructed of sections welded, instead of riveted, together and designed for a life of five years. They were named Liberty ships as Franklin Delano Roosevelt, the United States president at the time, said they would bring liberty to Europe.

These ships suffered hull and deck cracks, and twelve of these early ships broke in half without warning with the loss of lives. Also, the ships were frequently overloaded, and some of the problems occurred during or after severe storms at sea that placed any ship at risk. More than 2,400 Liberty ships survived the war and Greek entrepreneurs bought 526 ships and started their fleets. George thought this is how the shipping magnates made their millions. They would buy these Liberty ships cheap, sail to other countries, load another cargo, and make a profit. Now they could purchase another Liberty ship, or build another vessel, and sail again. Some of the ships sank, and the insurances paid top dollars, although the crew got nominal compensation, and if anyone complained, a Communist label awaited him.

11

Facing Death

On George's next trek, he flew to Belgium and boarded the *S.S. Telemon* and sailed from Norway bound for Baltimore carrying mineral in the hold. At 1,200 miles northwest of England and south of Iceland and Greenland, a huge storm hit. The menacing clouds darkened the sky, and the mammoth, stormy, tumultuous and turbulent thirty—foot waves assaulted and tossed the ship back and forth, like a seesaw, immersing the prow and then the stern under water. Finally, the ferocious, agitated storm cracked the ship, although it did not sink, but separated the deck from the bridge, the forward part of the ship's superstructure from which the ship is navigated, and the angry ocean poured into the deposit of fresh water. The frightened, anxious and apprehensive sailors did not sleep for three days and nights, but they recited prayer after prayer, and George became more religious than before this adventure.

The captain telegraphed the office in England, and was instructed to sail to the British Isles, but the next day the office telegraphed him to go to the Azores Islands, about 800 miles off the coast of Portugal, for repairs. After a week of restorations, the ship departed once again for Baltimore from the Azores. However, it seemed like Poseidon, the god of the sea, was not appeased, and it stormed afresh with such violence that the bow of the ship repeatedly sank into the cold, dark waters submerging half the vessel, while the stern rose up above the ocean. Once more, the ship cracked a second time at the same place, although still seaworthy, and needless to say, the crew once again was seized with sudden, violent alarm and terror.

Somehow, the ship made it to Baltimore, moored at the harbor for repairs anew, and the crew unloaded the cargo. Because they almost lost their lives, a few of sailors decided to leave this ship and take another one. However, the captain did not want to lose his assemblage and signaled to the immigration officers not to let them leave. When the immigration officers examined George, he saw out of the corner of his eye that the captain motioned them to deny him leave, so when they asked him if he would return to the ship, he gave an affirmative reply. On Saturday the crew worked half a day, and then they were free, so George worked until noon and told the immigration officer that he would go for a drink and return at 8:00 p.m. This time, George decided to "jump" ship, i.e., that is, leave the ship, so in spite of not being able to collect his pay, as this would betray his intention, he doubled his clothes, put on two extra pairs of underwear, extra shirt, pants and jacket before he disembarked.

12

Rest and Relaxation

It was February 1953, and George had time to visit relatives that lived in Pittsburgh now, so he met a friend, whom was recommended to George by another Ikarian, and who would help him get on a bus. They went to a movie until it was time to depart, at a time when he would not have to change buses from Baltimore to Pittsburgh. George boarded the bus and arrived in Harrisburg about 3 o'clock in the morning. The driver announced that he had to take another bus in fifteen minutes. Even though George had absolutely no knowledge of English, somehow he understood. He had only $25.00 in his pocket, and he went to the cafeteria, did not buy anything, but came out every minute to see if the other bus arrived.

Finally, it did, and he was the first to get on; when he arrived in Pittsburgh, he did not know how to get out of the station. He saw a door and went in, but it turned out to be the washroom; then, after looking around, he saw the stairs and got out. He saw a taxi parked with the driver asleep, and George knocked on the window and startled the driver, and at the same time he showed him the address where he wanted to go. George's aunt told him that it was about a ten minute ride to the house, but it took much longer, and George worried that the driver's intention was to rob him. Although no language exchanged between them, the taxi driver delivered him to his destination for a $2.00 fare.

Albeit was 6:00 a.m., still dark and cold, George did not want to wake up his relatives, so he sat on the door stoop. About this time the neighbor policeman exited from his house to go to work, and George became alarmed that he would spot him and arrest him, so he pretended to read the newspaper. In the meantime,

George's aunt and cousin went looking for him at the train station, and of course, did not find him, so they came home.

George's relatives welcomed him with open arms and with an ulterior motive of match making, introduced him to a couple single ladies, and he asked for the hand in marriage of one of them. The truth was George was now an illegal alien in the country; he had to marry a United States citizen so he could stay in the United States legally. One of the women agreed, so they prepared for the wedding, although this preparation paled compared to his previous failed betrothal in Athens, Greece, where the ceremony comprised half the liturgical event. In any event, George did not have the document from Greece that he was single; thus, the prospective bride's mother objected, and that was the demise of this courtship. With the second lady, no chemistry occurred between them, though George said he wanted to get to know her better; however, she indicated she had her mind on another suitor, thus this matchmaking also failed.

George was used to large cities in his travels, and was not particularly awed with the large cities in the United States, but now came to another metropolis, Cleveland, Ohio, to visit distant relatives, where he met the love of his life at a Greek picnic sponsored by the Pan-Ikarian Brotherhood, a non-profit, charitable organization of fellow Ikarians. He called the girl's mother, as her father was deceased, and asked for her hand in marriage. Marriages were arranged this way in Greece, and the custom continued in America; thus the intended bride of Ikarian descent agreed, and they were married in a week.

Now, George returned to Greece, and according to the law, his wife petitioned for him to enter the United States legally. Again, he encountered obstacles to this endeavor as well, since he served time in the English camp, because the soldiers objected to having King George return to Greece, and they were all labeled as Communists. Remember, George, at only 17 years old when inducted into the Army, had no political savvy or opinion. He never embraced Communism, a theory or political system that abolishes private ownership, that is, a society based on common ownership of property. He did not know the meaning of it, but during the 1950's McCarthy era most everyone was suspect.

The United States Senator Joseph McCarthy conducted inquiries into allegations of Communist subversion and espionage in the United States government and defense industries, as during the Cold War tensions fueled widespread Communist subversion. The Cold War was a period of East-West competition, tension and conflict, short of a full—scale war. Despite being allies against the Axis powers during the War, the United States was opposed to the Soviet Union's communism, and the Soviet Union had an anti-democratic view of the United States. With all of this, it took George eleven months to untangle the red tape, and then he had his beloved wife in his arms again.

13

A New Life

N ow, you would think it would be smooth sailing from now on. Nonetheless, George did not know the language, did not have a trade or higher education, and of course, he did not have employment. He got a job in a Greek restaurant as a dishwasher for $5.00 a day, and then at the advice of his brother-in-law, he applied at the Warner & Swasey factory, a leading manufacturer of machine tools. The company had a world-wide reputation for its telescopes and precision instruments and was best known for its astronomical telescopes and turret lathes, a machine that holds any material at both ends and turns it for shaping by a cutting tool. On his first day, his supervisor told him to get the broom and the wheelbarrow to sweep the floors. George answered, "Yes, yes," to all of his directives.

Finally, the flabbergasted supervisor told him "Yes, yes, but you do not understand anything!" He dismissed him and told him to go to school and learn some English. George heeded his advice and signed up for English lessons at Lincoln High School in the evenings. Learning English was difficult for George as his vocal patterns were set. He found it arduous to differentiate the sounds in words such as "seat" and "sheet," and could not understand why some letters were "rolled" such as "tt" in "butter" or the "d" in words such as "cedar," which were pronounced like an "r."

The silent letters in words such as "knife" also baffled him, because in the Greek language every letter is pronounced, and there are no long and short vowel sounds, so that if you know the sounds of the letters, you can read Greek. George returned to Warner and Swasey a month later, and the supervisor hired him this time as a sweeper for $2.00 an hour. Eventually, he earned more money, and he always thought of his parents and periodically sent them money. In the meantime, he studied for and received his United States citizenship, and consequently petitioned for his brothers to immigrate to the United States. Eventually all four brothers were together again, and his parents obtained visas to visit.

After about a year, the poor economy forced him out of work again. Doesn't this sound familiar? One and a half years passed before he got a job as a dishwasher again at a restaurant earning $30.00 a week. After a year at this job, Warner & Swasey recalled him, and George told his boss at the restaurant that he was leaving, but his boss told him to stay on, and promised him a better job as a cook. So, he stayed, and after he received another notice from Warner & Swasey and then a telephone call from them to return to work, George confronted his boss both times, and his boss reiterated his promise to make him a cook. George believed him, but this never happened, and he lost his chance to return to the factory as well as his seniority there. He tried to go back, but the opportunity was gone, and he returned to his dishwashing job.

George got a job at another restaurant and learned how to cook, but this lasted three months. After that, he got hired at a brewery, paid his union fees and dues, and at the end of twenty-nine days was laid off once more. Then the brewery hired new workers so they also paid union fees and dues. He worked another time as a cook at a restaurant and then at the Cleveland Hotel, now known as the Renaissance. By this time his three children, as well as his wife, raved about his cooking, and the children always knew who cooked dinner.

Eventually, George hired at General Electric as a sweeper, and after sweeping for two years, he was given the opportunity to take a test as a mechanic. He passed the test with flying colors at 100 percent, and after working for twenty-five years, retired. So George was blessed with his family of three children, seven grandchildren, and one great-grandchild and celebrated his fifty-fifth wedding anniversary in July 2009. He knew the value of an education and encouraged his children to seek higher learning, so that they could have an easier life than his. His wife became a teacher, while earning her Masters Degree in Education, and both his sons became engineers. His daughter got her degrees in business management and electronic data processing and earned her black belt in Isshinryu karate and taught martial arts. He says he is blessed to live in the greatest country in the world, loves to garden, hunt, and bowl and also does woodwork. George finally found that better life he dreamed about so long ago.